BI

# *Beating on Iron*
## *Kim Soo-Bok*

*Translated from the Korean by Brother Anthony of Taizé*

Barbara - George
love
Anthony

GREEN INTEGER
KØBENHAVN & LOS ANGELES
2016

GREEN INTEGER
Edited by Per Bregne
København / Los Angeles

Distributed in the United States by
Consortium Book Sales and Distribution (Perseus Books)
Distributed in England and throughout Europe by
Turnaround Publisher Services
Unit 3, Olympia Trading Estate, Coburg Road,
Wood Green, London N22 6TZ, 44 (0)20 88293009
ON NET (PDF) available through Green Integer
www.greeninteger.com
Green Integer
6210 Wilshire Boulevard, Suite 211
Los Angeles, CA 90048 USA

First Green Integer Edition 2016
English language translation copyright ©2016
by Brother Anthony of Taizé
Published in English by agreement with Kim Soo-Bok
Back cover material ©2016 by Green Integer
All rights reserved.
*Beating on Iron* is published under the support of the Literature
Translation Institute of Korea (LTI Korea). The publisher and
translator thanks LTI for their help in making this book possible.

Series Design: Per Bregne
Book Design and Typography: Pablo Capra
Cover photograph: Kim Soo-Bok

LIBRARY OF CONGRESS IN PUBLICATION DATA
Kim Soo-Bok (1953)
*Beating on Iron*
978-1-55713-430-1
p.cm –Green Integer 205
I. Title II. Series III. Translator: Brother Anthony
Green Integer books are published for Douglas Messerli
Printed in Canada on acid-free-paper

# Contents

From:
*Ballad of Mount Jiri, 1977*

# Snowstorm in Sancheong

Snow flurries fall close to the inn's lamp.
The beloved house is buried. The road is buried.
Songs for annihilation are buried too.
Stars flicker over the riverside's sandy reaches.
The beloved house is dragged off.
A few stretches of road are dragged off.
Dragged off. Dragged off. Shouts.
Songs for dragging off are dragged off, too.

# Jiri Mountain

A bird flying up over Granddad's grave
cries as it goes.
No news of Uncle though late azaleas bloom
  bright
then fall.
In the shadow of the falling flowers
Father's faint face fades.
He was massacred during the war.
On every ridge clouds are on the verge of tears,
borne along on the night bird's sobbing.
Westward. Westward.

# On the Shore at Yeonan

*Hwang Jini 2*

Hey, men; hey, men!
Come toward the sound of waves billowing on
the shore at Yeonan.
Kick aside the sadness of falling winter snow,
shake off the weak heart of azaleas, bush clover,
come floating lightly to a rock-firm island in the
West Sea.
All alone I have come to Yeonan, my body cast
aside,
and am watching the sunset glow suspended
above the sea.
Hey, men; hey, men!
Come toward the sound of waves driven by the
winter wind.
Here is someone with sorrows,
hung aloft like a lamp at Gwanghwamun
crossing,
my fragile flesh pierced by spear-like winds,
my ears slashed and slashed by blade-like
sorrows,
so share them out.

# Landscape Notes

A leaf fell,
news ended.
In empty fields
rooks formed flocks
and tore at the sunset.
An old peasant's funeral hearse
shunned the twilit sky.

From:
*Waiting for the Birds, 1989*

# Our Age's Lyric Poetry

Sitting on a hill in an autumnal grove of paint-
ed maples that had grown calm at afternoon's quiet
voice, I watched as demonstrators dispersed into
low stars. A few, borne on the wind, went and sat
in the shade within the grove, and I could see the
backs of a few others going into newly rising eve-
ning stars.

I also began to see that the little path leading up
into the wood was trying hard not to be jostled by
the wind, taking a tight hold of the meadow.

As soon as the path could be seen nearby, we
were both obliged to stand up again and walk be-
neath the crimson-flaming autumn sky until our
ankles ached.

# Kim Su-Yeong

That winter I lived in a rented shack in Oksu-dong and every night was kept awake by evil spirits and the couple next door fighting. I feared the nights. The evil spirits swept through my forest of deep insomnia carrying sharp-bladed spinning sickles, while the couple went on fighting till dawn.

Still not asleep as day dawned, when I looked out through my small window at the hillside track running up the hill, I saw it was frowning even though snow had fallen. I could see unmelted snow looking out at the world. That winter, tormented by poverty and insomnia, was full of shame.

# Flute Holes

My Grandfather's words, "If you want be be a bamboo, don't become a spear, become a flute," had come out to the lakeside by the hill behind the house. The paulownia tree in front of the house, that had slept fitfully the previous night, its back sweating slightly, had come out beside Grandfather's words. The bamboo grove that Grandfather had planted back when he was living in hiding here, perhaps during the Donghak uprising, was being shaken in the lake, stirring up waves. While the grove was being shaken by the wind, Grandfather was standing in the clamor that had once rung across the winter meadows.

At dawn today, beside the sleepless paulownia tree in front of the house I saw a few stars emerge from the flute holes and rise into the sky. My Grandfather's words, "If you want be be a bamboo, don't become a spear, become a flute," shook the hill behind the house until it woke.

# Afternoon Sleep

Your pretty toes have escaped from an afternoon doze and are dipped in streaming sunshine. The sea surging at the tip of your toes, then from toes to knees, from knees to thighs, to belly, the breast, your, your, breathing freedom

Listening to your free breathing, crossing your brook with its meandering stream, our shadows borne on our heads, we sink toward the sea, the tips of your toes, to knees, to thighs, to belly, to breast, to the forest of your breathing freedom…

# Before a Bush Fire

We stand here, this mountain's
October trees, settled, scarlet,
watching an evening bush fire
as it winnows the darkness, swallows the pain.
You, I, we lie here, one
unscorched, soaked field path
watching the far side of history
gradually cooling, hot.
Looking out at the darkening river
still faintly visible
as the end of frostfall dawn
sends the early morning birds flying.
We have so far not abolished this world's
        darkness,
only wandered like watery streams,
so how can you or I stand
as October's trees, not yet blazing,
linger after moistening our feet at the edge of the
        crimson-tinged sea?

# Daedun-san Mountain

The students stood like October's burning trees
proclaiming that they were uniting their
    solidarity, their human bonds.
I stood like a thirty-four-year-old tree
having no partner or generation to unite with.
They sang songs of love,
surrounded with blazing flames,
eyeing the partner each had in mind,
but I had no partner to indicate a song
and nobody who would stand up and sing if I
    called their name.
The students stood kindling a fire at the heart of
    an age,
proclaiming that they were uniting their love and
    bonds
but thirty-four-year-old I
was a thirty-four-year-old tree burning lonely
that could do nothing but gaze out at the West
    Sea.

# Waiting for the Birds

April went its way, April's love likewise went its
    way.
In the sleepless streets where magnolias fell
we waited for the birds.
Waiting for singing birds
we prayed.
While the sun shone bright for three days
we asked forgiveness for our sins
and waited for the birds.
We waited for praying birds.
The forest we dreamed of was too far away
and the sleepless night only grew deeper.
In the forest where April went its way and
    April's love grew deeper,
as we waited for singing birds
we prayed all day long
and in April's forest
we talked about the hope that did not return.

# Praying Trees

A voice saying, "All of you, be wakeful,"
echoed beneath olive trees growing all alone.
The olive trees grow ever more watchful,
and standing at April's end
pray for April's hope,
pray until day dawns,
pray for the tears of the morning star
until the shadows of despair are effaced,
shine out as praying trees
for the sleepless dawn road's revolution,
from morning till evening
from despair to hope
they stand as wakeful trees.

# Underneath the Spindle Tree

The pain stays the same though spring has come.
Though I survived last winter's icy winds
by rubbing my body
the pain stays the same—
the way sleep still will not come,
the way my nerves are on edge.

The moonlight settling on my shoulders seems
    painful,
the bellflowers visible at the foot of the next-
    door house's garden wall,
the spring nights that make petals droop and
    grieve,
the pain stays the same.

The heated words in the heart that keep bursting
    out,
last winter's snow flurries that suddenly grow
    chill when I sleep
and rise abruptly in my body
melt away when I awake at dawn.

But once the season comes that matches my

body's color,
once that comes, I'll go out into the streets and
all year long
I'll stand singing a song that matches my color.

# Hidden Face

Although darkness was thickening outside the
    window,
my daughter was absorbed in a picture puzzle.
The last image to be found
was the face of a helmeted warrior.

The picture, like the dark outside,
seemed determined not to yield,
while outside the April window leaves were
    falling.

Among the hidden pictures,
tree, sword, spear
were awake in the circles my daughter drew on
    finding them
but now night was falling with the helmeted
    warrior unfindable
and my daughter was growing increasingly
    fretful.

Amidst the unyielding dark,
trapped in the hidden pictures,
April's unsleeping face

the helmeted warrior's face did not appear till
    nightfall
as my daughter grew increasingly impatient.

From:
*Another April, 1989*

# Another April

April has come once more.
Students we had been without news of returned.
Friends appeared, smiling.
The red peach in front of the house put out fresh
    buds.
In our spring night, that had been tossed with
    nightmares,
the morning star shone out again.

It looks as though the stars we had been waiting
    for have come back too.

Once again April's dawn has come
and I have a new daughter.

# Beating on Iron

I will cast off the old dream of becoming
    president.
I will cast off last summer's burning desire
to make weapons' shadows in order to become
    president.
I will cast off the claustrophobic spring days
ramming April sunlight
into the weapons' shadows in order to become
    president.
Beating on iron, overcoming our age's
    increasingly red-hot hostility
within April's body
I will forget childhood summer evenings
when I used to say I would become president.
Beating on iron, I will become a hoe plowing up
weapons' shadows.

# Dew

My life will roll on
past the dew
hanging on plum trees at spring dawn.

Spring light will draw near
under plum trees' shadows.

You, spring sky,
unattainable though I offer up my life.

From:
*Praying Trees, 1989*

# Autumn River Autumn Song

In this deep autumn
we are the blazing red heart
of a maple forest.

We are the burning heart of autumn leaves
cherishing each other as they hasten clustered
through distant hills, distant clouds.

A single body, a single heart
from Halla to Baektu,
warm autumn songs
sung supported by one another.

And we are your autumn river
bathing last summer's hot wounds.

The wooly clouds beyond our bodies,
passing over hills
are the aching hearts
of our divided fellow-countrymen.

Beyond this autumn road we are taking
the autumn maple forest

blazing as one body one heart
is crossing beloved hills.

Within us
lies our autumn
that we embrace and dream of.

There is an autumn road that we must take
before we sleep.
There is the autumn forest,
we becoming ourselves.

Within us is an ever-deepening
autumn river.

Not crying out though we overflow,
not keeping silent though we blaze,
We are an ever-deepening autumn song.

# Mount Geum in Namhae

I have decided not to become
a piercing star again.

My youthful autumn road
is thus blazing bright

I have decided not to become
a road trembling in longing.

I have decided not to become that tossing
    evening sea,
death and love combined.

# Hail

Unable to settle
on those tossing winter trees,
on the lights in the streets at nightfall,
on the rear view of warm people,
on songs of hope,
on longing,
on the peace on more distant lands,
you unsleeping speckled stars
unsinkable.

# At Easter

Once evening Mass for the Sunday of the fourth week of Lent was over, I remembered the sermon about how "if one grain of wheat does not rot it remains merely a single grain of wheat." One grain of wheat became a tree, became the April sky, became the April sea. As I passed the statue of the Virgin in front of the church to the west in the direction the birds' shadows were vanishing I saw one red peach tree shaking in the garden. The birds left, flying into the twilight in rows, and the red peach tree that kept growing up and up into the heart of the twilight, where one grain of wheat was rotting, spoke with a strong voice. Evening Mass for the Sunday of the fourth week of Lent ended with the shadow of the hill in front, and the flight of the vanishing birds, and the growing peach tree in front of the altar. As I came down the church steps I saw a few stars shine then vanish in the middle of the cross.

# While We Sleep

We must not fall asleep.
While we sleep the snow
will fall more thickly.
Our forests will sink more firmly
into the twilight.

We must not fall asleep.
While we sleep the river
will have flowed on so far
and our birds
will cross the darkening woods and fly away.

We must not fall asleep.
Until the dawn forest wakes
and meets the river on it way to the sea
until the birds fly away
and become the melody of the red glow at
    nightfall.

From:
*All the Roads are Singing,*
1999

# Cold Mountain

Though Father has gone to heaven he has no house. In this world too he had no house. His house was in the flow of time. While I was born and grew up and went to school, Father had no house. When I graduated and wanted to dress him in my gown and mortar board he was embarrassed and avoided being photographed. He thrust the family tree among the other books deep inside the wardrobe and seeing my expression suggesting we should make a genealogy he would just gaze up at the sky through the window. In his eyes the pomegranate tree he had pruned used to be wrapped in twilight.

As we were coming out after burying Father in the Catholic cemetery, the snow stopped. The day grew bright again but inside me thick snow was still falling. Father had appeared the previous night in a dream, taken me by the hand, and as we went up to the second-floor Chinese restaurant at the market entrance, said he wanted a drink before he went. Waking with a start, I saw that rough snowflakes were still lingeringly falling outside the window.

# Fleabane

Why didn't I realize?
First driven into the sunlight of a late spring day
then suddenly forced up onto a hilltop,
didn't I end up sitting by the river in early
    summer?
At last
the sun set in the West,
and I brushed past
into the surging evening's twilight glow.

# April Letter 5

*Flowerbed*

One small flowerbed
lives deep down in my heart.

Violets and bellflowers,
just right for April's springtime light,

revering this land like heaven,
serving the people as masters,

in the peninsula's early spring dawn
arose, hands held high, and settled there.

# Winter River

The winter river flowed past behind my back.
After crossing the wrinkled folds produced by
     time
it blended into the reed beds
then began to sing
after which it flowed round the foot of the
     moonlit hills.
Sometimes it threw itself onto beds of gravel
and if it met a deep mountain would embrace it,
but also knew how to grow agitated and turn
     away.

When it pressed its flesh against the ferry
     landing,
cheered by the whispering sound
people began to rock their shoulders in a joyful
     dance.
Sometimes at dawn, coming near a village,
it would rub its chilled back against the banks,
or follow the footsteps of people entering the
     village
and flow into the yards of family dwellings;
it might also turn into a lamp over the threshold

of an isolated house
or the funeral lamp outside a house in mourning.

From:
*The Vanished Waterfall, 2003*

# Attic Room

*Sky lodging 1*

After moving into the attic room I did not go outside for several days. Sounds of rain knock at my heart while sometimes birds toss out news from far away as they pass. The way down to the earth's surface is too long, stairs only lead up to the sky.

If I just rest a few days, a few trumpet-creeper flowers will fall, the pneumonia in the clouds will cool the flames in passing and the twilight glow of wounds standing far away will sink beyond the western hills.

I long to rest for a few days, turning everything round and sending it down, washing bare feet alone, shutting doors, climbing up and down a few levels of sorrow, listening to the sound of streams, of leaves brushing together, of thunder rolling in the distance, and the footsteps of showers that once pursued me.

The winter I spent in that attic room in the Milky Way Inn up an alley in Bangsan Market on Uljiro 5, with its empty chair and occasional phone calls, the labyrinths within the silence I could not turn outside, the locked-in sorrows, the scorching stairs I kept longing to go down, the vast open air I kept longing to throw a stone into but never went to touch, with the windows that could not be opened, or rather without any windows, where I used to hide deprived of a shadow, or rather used to run long distances embracing a scorching shadow, where I could not tell someone I loved that I loved them, where the only thing I kept saying was: I don't know, I don't know, I don't know, but where every night I used to gaze up at the sky from the roof where the Milky Way flowed, that attic room in the Milky Way Inn.

After moving into the attic room I was sick for several days. Sounds of rain knock at my heart while sometimes birds toss out news from far away that I had forgotten as they pass through the sky. Outside, the now flowerless trumpet creepers are coming up the old stairs.

# Autumn Mountain 1

Now,
on my body too,

flowers blossom then fall,
clouds linger then pass on.

The places where once were green wounds
that burned brightly away

the sound of late evening streams
that once released pink ashes

at last seem to be heading seaward
after wandering far from their bodies.

Trees lighting fires
in each other's breasts,
calm their breathing,
calm their heavy breathing.

# Springtime Body-Flowers

Mother left after a visit.
In my heart
that cloudy spring day
a closed door opened
and on spring trees
body-flowers began to sprout.
An intense lilac fragrance
came strolling
into my melancholy body.

In Mother's body
far away could be heard
a bell ringing at dawn
birds singing as they flew through groves
the sound of a stream's ever lighter body
the sound of a blanket at dawn
as stars tossed then fell asleep
the sound as the first snap-weed petals
kissed the morning dew,

the sound of the footsteps of the first snow
falling at a mountain's foot.

Mother was standing behind my back.
That evening with wisteria blooming
resounded with the smell of soy sauce being
    boiled,
the grassy smell of children's bodies.
In the sunset glow, nothing but charcoal
    remained.

There was a bus belatedly winding round the
    curving hills,
a hill with a low cloud pressed down on its brow,
friendly roads surrendering their narrow bodies
    to one another,
trees that feel no sorrow even when the sun sets
    behind western hills,
an evening stream descending after washing
    itself.

Now flowers began to bloom
on my body.
Even in the cloudy spring day evening
the flowers did not wither.

# Days of Pilgrimage

I fled
from Father.
Outside was wonderful,
wild,
snow falling,
and outside all the sleeping villages
sleepless
streamsides.

A human being is heaven indeed.

The market-place with dust blowing,
the mountainside no carts returned from,
and as the smell of sesame leaves faded away
my heart looked up
at the collapsing sky
I walked till dawn.

Falling,
rising again,
day-break wounds,
pain descending below my knees.

A human person was not heaven at all.

I walked and walked.
Clouds went by overhead.
Rain fell.
People took shelter from the rain.
I stood there, caught in the rain.
While silver poplars stood in the rain all day
    long
rain likewise fell on birches' sorrowing skins.

I fled even farther
from Father.
In order to efface the birches' purity,
to efface the day-break wounds,
I hastened toward the sunset.

# Far Too Long an Autumn Road

One autumn, some forty years ago, there was one beautiful person who used to keep looking up at the sky, leaning against the young back of a plane tree. There was one autumn fellow who used to smear his face red with the greasy back of his hand as he leaned against the door of an old bus wielding an oily rag. The road that went from Chungmu-dong to the hilltop terminus in Yeongseon-dong, embracing red leaves, was far too long, as long as next autumn's arrival.

# The Vanished Waterfall

On the slopes of the hill behind our village nestled a little lake. Every time the lake's heart grew heated, it would send down the hill a little of its heart in a low voice.

We children, standing on the path leading up the hill, used to call those songs flowing down in a low voice "the little waterfall." We would set up a parasol below it and sing as we bathed our feet.

One summer, a few writers spread out a straw mat below that "waterfall" and drank liquor; they shouted at the people in power that summer, poured out in strong voices the heated songs within their hearts.

Then at some point the little waterfall disappeared.

The bare rock, its breasts dried up, lay naked and the low, soft voice could not be heard.

The lake's body too grew gaunt, and though its body would soften as rain fell on summer evenings and it would sing songs of faint memories, the melodies did not come flowing down.

It changed into gray garments that did not suit it and, once it was wrapped about with barbed wire to keep people out, its body grew even more gaunt and its heart no longer grew heated.

Once it could no longer sing songs on moon-lit nights, the waterfall's strong voice died and went to heaven, then at dawn it would rub tears into the rocks' dried-up breasts in a voice devoid of strength, that voice dying with the sunrise and going back to heaven.

# Masan-po

There is no more sea now in Masan-po. There is no evening sea, that used to soak ankles in the yard of the wharfside house, the mist gathering on the road to the evening sea that lies sprawled, its ample breast exposed, that used to come pouring eagerly in.

The evening sea at Masan-po that used to shine on distant islands, sharing with the islands' very heart, and people, after bathing in the waves' soaking songs until evening when the tide came in, returned as inland bodies embracing the sea, but now no one returns.

The Masan-po sea that used to soak the ankles of birds between the reed beds behind the backs of departing boats rocking in the wind, the Masan-po sea that was never angry though people returned embracing the sea then failed to return, the Masan-po sea now has only dry teats, having lost those breasts that were once so bashful.

The Masan-po sea that cannot now suckle distant waves and the new moon, the Masan-po sea where between the reed beds, stroking the dry wind's face, birds used to go falling into the evening sea's breast and die then spread as the twilight glow.

The sea lies drained of blood, an empty shell, unable to rise.

# Autumn Crosses Mountains

Once it approaches fifty, the body turns into an autumn mountain. Hugging its crimson-hued breast, the body grows heavier, blue bruises remain here and there and the ridges of old scars stand out strongly, while it sometimes sends the trees and leaves that toss between the thick mists surging and winding round its ankles flowing down to a lower place.

After waving from afar at the peak, weary, fainting, the bent-backed roads lie flat below the clouds. The heart grows ever hotter as it crosses the mountains. Breast strikes breast; reclining, a pink mist wraps the roads on the peak as it penetrates the sky's womb, then riding its body it crosses over. The bodies of pink clouds soaked in sweat blossom crimson abundantly.

# Cheomseongdae

*Handkerchief Painted with*
*the Heavenly Horse 1*

After making a turn round Cheomseongdae,
looking at Cheomseongdae as it stood waiting for
someone, I bought a handkerchief painted with
the heavenly horse at the entrance to the Heav-
enly Horse Tomb.

On the heavenly-horse-painted handkerchief, a
single birch tree with lovely bark had long
been standing.
Though it said: Go back, it's time to go back, I
did not go
but stood holding the reins of my heart.

People came crowding then vanished, the sun
set, evening came,
the time came for the woods to sleep but the
single birch stood until its body grew dark.

Though old, looking up at the sky, just looking
at Cheomseongdae as it stood there,
saying: It's alright if I die, just being able to
look, it's alright if I die,

the single birch tree had long been standing.

*Note:* Cheomseongdae is an ancient stone tower in the former Silla capital of Gyeongju. The Heavenly Horse Tomb is one of the royal tombs not far from the tower; in it was found a wooden saddle painted with a flying "heavenly horse" which gave it its name.

# A Snapweed Letter

*Handkerchief Painted with
the Heavenly Horse 3*

On the coast of Siberia, at the navel of an old hill, a snapweed was blooming on a distant cliff that no hand could reach. Early one morning before the sea had opened its eyes I emerged from the dormitory of the Naval College and was gazing intensely at the snapweed's round breast.

It told me that snapweed was also blooming by the brushwood gate through which I had left my home aged twenty, when the hot moon had departed from my breast.

In its green and red eyes, that drew me the more I gazed, I could see dewdrop tears saying: You took such a round-about way, you have only now arrived, could you still not receive the letter launched on the waves escaping from your breast?

# River

*Handkerchief Painted with
the Heavenly Horse 4*

When the moon was full, Lake Baikal put its heart's rough waves to sleep within, entered its fully pregnant body, sent the umbilical cord far away and made a river.

Riding on moonlight,
the river
passed birch woods,
crossed sleeping villages

passed plains,
reached the distant dawn sea

gave birth to islands
one by one
then came back again.

# When Lilac Falls

They will say the ways they trod were beautiful,
and will not forget.
The spring that ended so soon, I cannot even
    recall its face,
climbing over the wall, hands outstretched,
    looking skyward together,
now will fall into that sea's center
and turn into an island.

# Island 2

The moment evening fell,
the sea
raised itself
and cooling crept stealthily
beneath the skirts
the camellia grove was dying red.

From:
*The Eye of the Well, 2004*

# Temple Hall

Inside my body
there is a temple hall.

Inside my body
where darkness gathers
there is a temple hall
that has long
been empty.

If I push open the ancient door
and go in
the sound of the road, that had been lying
before the old door, stands up,

trees laying down on the ground
heavy burdens
and once again lighting
bud-lamps in their hearts,

birds
waking from long sleep
and flying again,

inside my body
there is a temple hall
where a dawn bell
rings again

# Pregnant Palm Tree

If you leave Mykonos harbor behind you, be-
yond the wall of Leto Hotel a single palm tree has
long been standing. Even when the wind blows it
does not shake, just listens to the distant sound of
the waves, standing until the sun declines, in the
memory of one island that cannot approach though
it is near. There is a woman who endures her preg-
nant body, waiting for the island to rise to the sur-
face. There is a palm tree that has long been stand-
ing, stomach full, until a church bell is heard and
a full moon rises. Until the round island within its
body is born.

# The Eye of the Well

Between the crumbling walls of back-alley houses in a ruined hilltop city there used to be an empty well. When evening came, inside the empty well where a few fig trees had rented space, shooting stars used to come falling and become the pupil in the well's eye.

They became the well's eye where they could for a long while scrutinize their image in the sky.

# Dead Wood

*Rules of Loving 10*

As I advance toward the foot of the mountain, lying there with its old body containing the mountain's inner spine, I contemplate the ancient interiors of the trees bathed in sunlight. I advance along love's ancient alleys.

# A Storeroom

People each have a storeroom inside them. There they can hide rusty nails picked up in the alley one evening, with squeaking stairs, hide desires, and silently deposit shoes wet from morning walks with dew, collect crosses, hide the sins everyone secretly commits, in the storeroom each one has inside them.

# Laughing

Mother, long confined to her sickbed, fell asleep once the sunlight escaped from her body then woke when I came late in the evening to visit her, and laughed.

Then she said to me:

"The sun looks more beautiful just before it says goodbye, doesn't it?"

The words softly murmured by the monk in the Himalayan White Deer Temple turned into a moist sunset glow and my eyes grew blurred.

# In a Corner

Sitting in a corner of a rooftop room in the Hotel Kimon facing the Parthenon, I gaze at the temple. The light in the temple gradually fades, the people suddenly vanish, and I start to think of my mother, wife and daughters, the house, the trees waiting for spring to come, the streams flowing through cloudy days, the fleabane flowers of silently approaching summer days, in a far-away country.

The tide of the demonstration against war, against the dispatch of troops, that is flowing through the square, ebbs away, sequestered midday returns.

I hear a church bell inside myself
calling me.

From:
*Walking After the Moon, 2008*

# Someone Said

Someone said:
if the leaves of trees fall off
and press their lips to the ground, it is so that
they may be reborn as baby trees,
so that their body's rainbow may be seen again.

Someone said:
if a grain of wheat does not fall to the ground
and rot,
it will remain a single grain of wheat and not be
    able
to bring into being the wind's fragrant forest it
  contains.

Someone said:
if the hill back home, despite time's passing,
spreads out the wide sky and stays lying there,
it's because the songs of birds that have not yet
    returned
still linger in its ears.

Someone said:
if we lean against one another,

and form a forest as we go on living,
it's because there is still a dawn
we have to sing.

Someone said:
if a river speeds on all life long then lays its
    body in the evening sea,
it's because it can hear tales of the love
the evening sea is unable to share,
because the sea has tales left that the hill could
    not finish,

because someone is still speaking.

# Fellowship

The flowering cherries in Wolmun-ri, Namhae,

when the moon rises from within the sea

stand up straight together

and at the sound of the moon passing

open wide their bodies' petals,

no matter if they die, no matter if they die,

they stop the moon's mouth

and until the sea shuts its door

scatter scales of death on the sea.

# Verdure

Mother is dressing me.
Stripping off the guilt,
black,
that once obliged me to cover my body with
    rocks,
nothing left but a husk
the gaunt
body imprisoned in darkness,
Mother is dressing me in new clothes.

# Winter Forest

Now my body has become a winter woodland,
bygone days' flesh has fallen away,
leaves have all fallen and will not return.
The wind blows between the bones within the
    wood.
At the branchtips of remote memories I once
    loved
evening has begun to lay its colors.
Someone is looking down at me.
Now I have sent away everything
that once dwelt inside my body, and as I gaze
into the empty well inside me,
the stars above my head I used to think beautiful,
the gaze of people I used to love as pale green
    leaves,
the enmities of narrow alleys, all those things
slip away, but someone is still looking down at
    me,
saying: the fight is not over yet.
With the distant evening glow penetrating my
    flesh
I am standing, my quite empty body glowing.
My body is standing torn and glowing.

# Mud Flats

She lies there with her hugely pregnant body.
At dawn a ship leaves, cutting through her
    stomach.
As it emerges from her body, headed for the sea,
trailing its umbilical cord,
oh, from within her body forcefully the innocent
    sun
is driven out and up.
Inside her empty body remain scattered shrouds,
nothing but head-towels women forgot.
Empty cockle shells that become feed for living
    creatures
become silent, empty midday houses.
A flock of speckled seagulls comes flying,
they force their way inside her body and fight
    among themselves.
Our mothers bore us
inside war-like bodies.
As evening comes, amniotic fluid bubbles up,
    the moon rises,
father returns from far away at sea.

# A Spring Day

A spring day
listening to the story emerging at noon from the
    radio,
about a girl who passed up university and took a
    job instead
because her brothers were already attending
    university,
bought presents for her mother and father with
    her first wages
then regularly sent home her monthly earnings
and her mother opened an account in her
    daughter's name,
went to the bank and paid in the money her
    daughter sent.

# Relationship

Jeondeung-sa temple has naked women carved
    in its eaves.
They crouch there with nothing on.
Pushing down with both arms, they are being
    punished.
The carpenter who built the temple imprisoned
    there
the woman who abandoned him.

# The Sea

*Barbed Wire Poems 1*

At last Hwaseong's Jeongok port has reopened.
Rusty barbed-wire had been wound all round it
but now the barbed wire has been removed
so that international boat races can be held.
Now it lies open, the tide rises, then in the
    evening the tide ebbs
and beyond it the sun sets.

One poet tried to sing of the setting sun escaping
over the distant sea beyond the barbed wire
but said his eyes stung so he slept fitfully.
Facing the evening that sings of peace, ships
    launched on the sea,
the sun goes down, into the darkened eyes of the
    barbed wire wrapping all,
unable to sing of the long evening after dark.

The bone that was long driven into my body is
    being caught again.
I am driving the rusty bone, once wrapped all
    round my body,
deep into the dimming twilight mud-flats.
I am driving in deep the song within me

that can cherish long the setting sun.
Until those fragmented songs become the sun
and rise again within my body.

# Silence

*Barbed Wire Poems 2*

Since I have received such a great blessing
I will now become a poor barbed-wire
    entanglement.

I will hide my face,
shy even of the wind's breath.
I will tell the stars emerging inside me
to rise lower.

I will throw a stone at the clouds
floating in the sky and tell them to shut their
    mouths.

I will send water to divided lands
and make them one.

Since I have committed such a great sin
I will slash my whole body,

cut out my tongue,
hang it on the twilight glow as the sun is setting.

# The Woods

*Barbed Wire Poems 3*

It was during our honeymoon days,
my wife was unable to fathom the fever within
    me
that sent me roaming in the woods,
returning late.
She used to roll over,
unable to fathom
the tears of poetry, just like my body,
after I talked of poetry
as I drank.

# Demilitarized Zone

*Barbed Wire Poems 7*

The moon's eye was all bashed in,
so that the bottom of the well was fully visible.
Stars go by,
drop one of their eyes,
the Demilitarized Zone.

From:
*Sleeping Out, 2012*

# I Go Walking into
# a Spring-Tree

Constantly inclined to start talking to anyone,

sitting idly in a room with the light out,

looking like eyes eager to blossom as us, not
    alone,

echoing long with whistles of birds somewhere
    mixed with sighs,

piercing earth's strata then waiting for the feet to
    grow hotter,

a bolt from the blue passing,

turning into the pupils of the eyes of utter
    darkness,

hugging your back then beaming broadly,

in the winter

that longed to close its eyes and go down
    endlessly to the bottom of a lake

then open its eyes and die,

I now go walking into a spring-tree

longing to start talking endlessly to the wind.

# To You Blossoming

Love's corpse spoke:

Beneath the best grown tree
the best rotted corpse is lying.

In the eye of the greatest love
can be found the pupil of the deepest sorrow.

From the spring tree to you blossoming.

# Memories of Laundry

Birdsong arises from each and every body.
It remembers the song of that thunder bird
that perched briefly one autumn evening,
the smell of the dead wind,
above the short, tough life
of the lightning that strikes dry skies,
above the poles of silence that laugh and flutter,
it remembers people's bodies.
Every time the wind blows, scattering
their anger and
their despair and
their labors and
their hopes and
their harms,
it listens to the sound arising from people's
    bodies.

# Jusanji Pond

It seems to have released into the empty air such
    a sad heart,
to have raised its body
toward the sky's breast,
and once raised up
it seems to have spent the whole winter.
It seems to have given birth to every silence
poised thus in the very center of the sky's breast.
It seems to have raised up the whole sky, and
    once raised,
to have planted there the roots of that distant
    past,
that distant past's love.

# I Turned Away, Pretending to Ignore

See how the reeds of Baekdam's Bukcheon
    stream,
out sitting along the streamside, are chuckling
    among themselves,

At times falling over, leaning on one another,
knocking and rubbing against one another,
lying there receiving the autumn sunshine's
    cares
soaking wet, as though nothing was wrong

Those staring pale white faces
are not so unpleasant,

I turned away, pretending to ignore the way
the Bukcheon willows, at their strongest, were
    standing upside down
stretching their roots toward the moon as it
    floated in the pools.

# God's Inn

Dear Lord! Already I am repenting.
Don't worry.
The funeral wove between the cherry blossom
and once the grave was finished
everyone went back home.
Lying now fallen here, covered
by dawn's blanket is good;
the pillow of solitude is good.
It has become the crying space
for all the birds and insects.
It has become the inn
where the shadow of the moon on its way to the
    eastern sky
stops to sleep.
It has become the friend of stars returning home
    late
in secret, sending them off turning and turning
after spending a night of human life.
Today again a man without sin gladly climbed
    up,
slept for a night in the room of expiation
and continued on upward.

# Home Port

One night, peeping at the mudflats
that never sleep,

see, giving suckle
to the shore off Chilsan

and gently offering the breast
to the new moon
that has woken at dawn and is fretting to be fed,

the full moon, our mother.

# An Alley

As soon as evening came it made the alley grow
    deeper

The alley, anesthetized,
its body abruptly locked in.

The peace in the alley has dropped by for a
    while.

Distant road

Furtive as intestines

There is a sound of feet
that once came and went happily or sadly.

Now that alleyway
has turned into house arrest,
every path leading home has been cut.

I deperately quit
the alley that the sunset glow is coloring.

Once out at the entrance to the alley
I expose falsehood
and cancer cells
and the past of all despair.

All past nationalism and capitalism
and socialism and Marx and Lenin and Mao Tse
    Tung
but Kim Gu and Sowol and Yun Dong-Ju,

But all wounds
are exits linking body to street,

In the alley
I dreamed of reason
and revolution, stood up to authority,
inside a solitary trashcan
I spat and spread mud over eyes.

Only eyes that were blind could be opened.

No sign of a way leading out,
and even the ways only leading in, those remote
solitary
ways in dreams that used to decapitate
oppression

Have now opened their eyes
and become far-away alleys.

# Sleeping Out

I think I'll rest a bit more before I set off, God.
A late-blooming wild flower is still a flower,
    surely?
How could I leave behind this fleabane
which has blossomed all its life long among the
    people in the alley?
Can't you see its unpowdered tears?
I am a flower, mother returning to life, that
    bloomed in this alley
at the foot of the wall of that old noodle shop,
and amidst all the people
a man-flower such as God likes blossomed too.
And those clouds, that approach, having
    nowhere else to go,
and those far-off waves of first love are still
    blooming, surely?
I will not leave before the sun falls quietly
    asleep
beyond the sea.
No matter how much you call,
until that man-flower blossoms in this alley,
I will not obey.
I want to go on blooming as a man-flower for

one more day,
just one day longer.

# Fossil Colored by Sunset's Glow

That's the way veins must have dried.
Tears with no more tears left,
the ardent sound of far distant wind
as a voice my ears cannot hear,
that long river's umbilical cord,
these I must have thrust up from within.

Tap tap, raising up a menopausal womb from
    underground,
squeezing, squeezing inside the body the sun
petrified above the distant ridge,
I must have obtained a seed.

Even though I turn to ash
spread out in the twilight glow,
displaying a millennial source of light
cherished as the setting sun,
like one leaf or two born open mouthed
I will come back to life as a dead body.

# A Cliff

Wondering if this is how I must die,
I watch a stream beating its breast as it slides
    and falls.
You, you
who once were hallowed by the wind's breath
as you came racing across the heart's plains,
for how many years now
have you set adrift petals falling thick
as you beat on your breast's drum, I wonder?
Maybe, taming the resentment surging hot like
    this
into such a very slow waterway
and stroking the cliff's breast
while licking the veins, thus, thus
dropping into the cave of despair
then scattering as the petals of a greater wind,
I might fall into the void?
I wonder how many stars have vanished
and turned into cliffs between man and man
destined to die beating their breasts?

# Sunrise Peak

## 1. Seven in the Evening

As soon as the sun began to decline,
darkness slowly veiled his eyes.

Old friend, if anyone asks,
tell them that I came to Jeju Island to die.

The setting sun trembled briefly.

The direction in which the sun was slowly
    sinking more deeply grew sad.

Only look at human history, old friend, don't you
    realize that world history
is a constant repetition of rulers exploiting the
    ruled?

I've come to die really well, I've come
to make my grave.

The sun dropped deep into silence.

All the world's silences are graves:
the words of the sun rang out as it set in
    darkness.

## 2. Indeed

I, because of mother, mother,
because mother was the cosmos,
because of all mothers who are summits of hope

because of thinking of that mother,
I was unable to leap into the flames

and went about scanning the hesitantly
    darkening alleys.
If I emerged into alleys where dawn was further
    off
the road's prison came before dawn.

Indeed, the road was a prison.

Like the grave of ideas
it made silence long, very long.

## 3. And So Silence Became Poetry

Having passed through Ojori, Naejoheon and

Chomak
I am writing down the poetry of silence.

The sun rises
before the grave of the man who said he had
    come here to die
whom I lament.

The black body welcoming inside itself
first of all the spreading light
is the brightening dawn

that stares up at the sun's gaze.

# A Navel

A furrow that a snake crawled into in a vegetable
    patch,
that the sun was sucked into and did not emerge
    from again

drawn along a dirt track
after a shower had passed, the departing sunset
    glow's

tail hid and did not emerge again,
that place.

# The Time a Lotus Stared at Me

There was a time when I wanted to bite the lobe
    of its ear.
I cursed the heavens,
even quarreled with the passing wind,

And when I realized that the lotus beneath my
    feet was staring at me
I bit the lobe of the lotus leaf's ear.

It was one late summer's evening
in Deokjin Park, that had returned to life after
    dying,
brightly.

Endlessly, endlessly I bit
so did not realize that dawn's lotus seeds were
    ripening.

# Daytime Moon

Crossing the ridge of Mount Umyeon, beside
    Yangjae stream
after looking at hawkweed,
then looking at yellow winter jasmine,
looking at weigela trees,
then looking at the back view of a cotton rose,
floating bare-faced in an empty sky,

ah, I see the daytime moon.

In my youth, if a daytime moon rose I would
    turn to daytime drinking
then wander alleys like nighttime paths.

Now the moon is following suit.
There, on the stone wall, become the mother of
    mother become a stone wall,
it is still following on behind.

One poet who is like the moon's gaze
says to come quickly to Mapo, the smell of
    autumn shad grilling is good.

Hearing the watery sound of the unknown
    guitarist
singing on the waterside stage, I hesitated.

The sun rises dark above a cemetery
and in the shadow, the shadow of the sun,
hidden in the shadow of every tear, inside the
    risen half-moon,

One heron, without moving from its place,
is gazing into its own body with its flowing
    stream.

Such so-called human life
is a matter of looking into one's sorrows,
gazing at one's prison,
gazing at one's revolution,
gazing at one's evening,
gazing at one's blazing love
until tears run dry!

Releasing the path one's heart must take
in any kind of rage, any kind of hatred,
any deep river.

In that way the daytime moon was looking down
    at me.

# A Tower

Evening will soon draw near.
Once the lamps are lit,
having offered its life
for the lofty and lowly dark
and the stars,
in the sky
that builds its home in the body
a bell will soon ring out.
Birds will die and fly away.

# The Trees are Sucking Milk from Graves

Now night seems to have fallen.
All the trees inside the body

enjoy the low hills,
recall the little paths through woods
and remote, carbonized women,
while night has fallen too on streams that dream
or spend the day walking,
or stand gathered laughing or weeping all day
     long.

Unable to become anyone's daily bread,
in the Bois de Boulogne
the trees are sucking belated time's milk.
Standing there after sucking the sun's milk,
they remember mother
vanishing into far-away forests.

All will enter that forest and die
while the morning sun will be reborn.

But in the benighted shop of human life,

not missing those people who departed, departed
     first,
not rejoicing at the sun that will be reborn,
in the forest of thick mists the trees
are sucking milk turned into graves.

# Sitting on the Chair of Time

I am sitting on the left-hand chair
in the Domenico Café, from where I can see the
    basilica of San Domenico.
I am sitting on that chair deep in time on which
    the poet of night beyond night,
Antonio Colinas, is said to have talked of poetry.
As the basilica is increasingly tinged with a
    crimson hue
it turns into an abundant hanging garden.
Flowers will bloom,
birds build houses,
and sometimes gypsies come in to sing.
Night cats will turn into hungry people
and try to get some sleep.
Let them sleep: the basilica
will speak and cover their impoverished bodies
with a blanket of the sky.
In order to gain forgiveness people will turn into
    donkeys
and ask for prayers.
Behold, your servant is here: they will shout
without realizing it.
Time's garden

in San Domenico monastery is slowly
	illuminated
then every evening
and daily silence
and gypsies turned into donkeys
and cats turned into servants
and aging trees
will turn into people
ringing the dawn bell
in the deep sky.
Sitting in the Domenico Café
I gaze at the basilica that has turned into people.

# Wuthering Heights

*In Salamanca*

In the sky, too, there is a low Wuthering Heights.
A place to hasten to and sit when tears flow,
a place for gazing endlessly southward as day
    breaks,
there's a hill that people have kept hidden inside
    them
where the wind blows at sunset

At the city's end, the sun falling and never again
    emerging.

Standing on the hill that gypsies call Wind,
waiting for the old sun of the twilight city
to set,
I listen to a year's worth of stories
sent from the South.
Becoming the gypsies' neighbor,
inside a heart that the sky gazes down on,

The city lights will become a witch imprisoned
    in a cave
and escape again from that alleyway.
Recalling the memories of cliffs

where winds rage and shake windows,
streams of tears endlessly pouring down,
alleys lying aslant in memories,
the eyes of low stars floating in the breast,
the gaze of the Wuthering Heights
sitting in the sky
quivers.

# Echoes

*In Patmos*

A shower falls inside my heart.
Moonlight follows behind the moon
as it climbs up the steps of the cave-church,
and *thud thud*, the sound of the distant sky's
    footsteps can be heard.

In my Oksu-dong days, the evil spirits that came
    crowding every night
pierced both my ears
saying: Listen to the sound of the wind.

I hear the fluttering voice
that hung a cross on the wall of the wind,
the voice of the wind I could not hear back then.

As I go up the steps echoing with the sky's
    smile,
that are like bones of sorrow stripped of fat,
I see birds vanishing into mother's breast.

The distant sea's sons now come back across the
    wave-tops,
and between the olive trees birds turn into stars

and rise again.

Dead forests awake and place lights on evening
    meal tables.
From far way, thunder passed by once more.

# A Monastery

Birds form flocks
that are driven into silence
and die

Full of graves,
the far, far away
evening sky

Beyond the window
thunder growls.

# A Donkey

When it tries to suck the setting sun's milk,
the sun kneels down
and lowers its body.
It sucks at the milk that has not emerged
from dawn
until dusk.

# Beautiful Stone

She followed behind me.
She followed, footsteps muffled by snow flurries
one evening when even the mountains held their
    breath.

But when I looked back there was nobody there.
Only the winter wind struck my breast.

Creating a stir in naked minds
that walked through the void.

Die, die: every night
falling asleep and dying
beside the stone sent from the sky
in Mirinae, by Bukcheon stream in Manhae
    Village near Baekdam temple,
that comes and flutters by my bedside at dawn.

Saying: Give me greater pain,
not deeper compassion,
kill me as a mere stone.

Turned into a living fossil

smouldering black,
she hurls herself
into that deep, scorching winter snow flurry.

# Dark Clouds at Noon

Passing over Akgyeon Mountain
they reached Mount Yubang.

The bones in their bodies began to itch.

Like shoals of minnows enamored of their hue
enjoying stream waters

passions too turned into cumulus clouds piling
    high at noon
rubbing soft hands on mountaintops.

After living a lifetime

They turned into rain and poured down
into valleys brimming with sunshine.

They stabbed down into hillside fields
crunchy with dry corncobs.

# Tangerines

Even when a baby was due, still we endured and
    went picking tangerines, you know;
grandmother and grandfather stroke the
    children's youthful faces and laugh.

# The Poet's Postface

# Writing Poetry in a Torrent

## 1.

Once I passed sixty, an occasional habit began of packing away one by one, as if pursued, my age, memories, the currents of life. Whether it was a letter found lying silently between the pages of a literary journal after I had been tidying up the books that all through the year had been piling up, pushing toward the stairs of my house, or dawn opening the door of daybreak and beckoning, or evening twilight long glancing back with pitying eyes, as I recall my eighty-year-old mother's voice on the phone saying, "I'm alright. Don't worry," increasingly often I have found myself gazing from afar at the scene as I dragged "me" far off and hurled myself down.

## 2.

How many battles of the imagination have I fought in order to escape from the torrents of the age in which I have lost myself, lost my soul, and in order to climb up a streamside hill to find the lyrical "I"? Now, quietly contemplating all day long the riddle proposed by the stream is enjoyable, the pleasure of poetry leading inside myself feels cozy. That is how the poem "On Reaching Sixty" came flowing into me. Waves of feeling that make spring rain, too, feel affectionate like a longtime lover, come flowing into me, into my breast, into some deep heart of my poetry, as I wait for spring days to come again, like a heart waiting for poplar-tree buds to emerge. Gestures pouring down and a smile bouncing up, like a lover long enduring and waiting for "me," have come flowing into the stream of my poetry.

3.

Sometimes too there were experiences of climbing the hill behind my home at sunset, sitting down on a seat in the shade of the hill, waiting for the far side of time, when the sun gave up the ghost. And there were infinitely many times when I loved the boundary between being's creation and destruction, repeating, "Over there, flowers are falling. Over there, far away, over there, flowers are drooping. On the inside and outside of all boundaries, far away, flowers are breathing their last."

I used to possess several power stations of romantic imagining in the very midst of an intense breast, that would measure the distance between intellect and sensitivity, between soul and flesh. Nowadays, far away, my heart's power stations, that once embraced one another passionately and gave light, are closing their doors one after another, shutting down. Rather than the electric shocks of passionate feeling, I have come to prefer love's power station that offers a warm hand, weak though it is when it comes to approaching a dark heart, lamplight illuminating a heart of darkness with a heart of light,.

4.

Now, the far side is visible. All this time, inside and outside have kept dreaming of becoming one body, a single body. The inside shook off and drove away the outside, sensitivity cast aside intellect, soul cast off body, and seems to have been waiting alone over there, far away, to become solitary. Perhaps only a soul waiting alone can be free? I even tried to believe that free, total freedom's destiny alone can make perfect the soul, the sensitivity, the you within me.

5.

Once the sun has fallen into the breast of the

far side of sky, going to that sky, going to the sky beyond that sky, whom might it be meeting? Dante followed Beatrice to heaven and met the Glory of Light, his eyes were blinded by that face, so did he set just the glory in the midst of his heart and become the sun? Did he escape from everything? Did he grow free from the love that robbed him of his soul? Repeating that, how many days did I spend wandering in youthful evening forests? Spreading clay on the eyes of poetry, how often did I pray that the world might be healed?

## 6.

Once a day I go to a neighboring art park and sit on a seat soaked in dawn. I gaze at love's figure, which is like the voices of the spirits of a silent forest, the voices of trees' confessions and the screams of birds. How earnestly did I long for my poems to have those confessional screams and leap with love's heart?

I also sometimes go and sit on a seat by the flowing ripples of the Yangjae Stream. How long did I spend, observing evenings of a long remaining gaze where moonlight fell, life's past journey recalled by that gaze, the alleys and currents once pierced by the rage of that black-and-white film?

Afternoons when I go and sit in the heart of the heron by Yangjae Stream, that very occasionally comes flying into my heart, are pleasing. As I sit on some seat of joy, the lonesome, honorable heron's lover comes briefly visiting, a fellowship making my seat of joy shake as though thunder-struck, and in the context of welcoming life's thrill, my poetry grows warmer, more rapturous.

7.

I have lived like the moon sleeping-out. Frequenting poetry's old flophouses, my poetry grew old. Dawn alleys linked endlessly to the world's markets, those alleys' multiple exclamation-marks of life, for how long, how very long have I been stuffing and pressing down in poetry's breast images of the intersecting gazes of people emerging from plazas, entering plazas?

My poetry's breast was a cave, it was Jeju Island's "Mureung Gotchawal cave." It was a flash of metaphors proposing to revive a ravine of dead roots, employing all its might, and by an imagination that entered the ground and raised it up, making dark clouds, making sudden showers, to revive all the ground's dead roots. Now, constantly extending as far as the distant sea, it was the languages of rainbows soaring into the sky. My poems!

## 8.

My "alley" brought healing. Having thrown a stone in the street, I took care of the pain of the age struck by the stone, that discord, after moving them into the alley. Wasn't the light at the end of the alley Mother's loving gaze, and the power of the myth that gave us regeneration, and the origin of the being who guarded us from the age's violence that robbed us of all reason for being? The poem "I Go Walking into a Spring-Tree" from my collection "Sleeping Out" was a lyric resurrection, finally forcing open the prison gates, having become an innocent lifer, and boldly walking out of the imagination of intense despair, an imagination like a Manchurian crane flying up embracing the egg of the sun. It was a switch turning off concepts and norms, until the day of liberation from the prison of language, that dreamed of meaning, the death and resurrection of meaning.

## 9.

Now, having cleared away the froth from the vortices of culture, devoid of any exit, unable to reach the sea, my poetry has become a stream intent on flowing free. I will protect the rhythm of the free waves from the rushing torrents of the age, from the muddy waters flowing down from higher up, from the side-streams accumulating in every heart. Calming the splashing sound made in the stomach by the traces of pain derived from the torrents, governing life's labor-pains, onward to the place where the rhythms and dance of my poetry's stream are leading!

GREEN INTEGER
Pataphysics and Pedantry
Douglas Messerli, *Publisher*

Essays, Manifestos, Statements, Speeches, Maxims,
Epistles, Diaristic Notes, Narrative, Natural Histories,
Poems, Plays, Performances, Ramblings, Revelations
and all such ephemera as may appear necessary
to bring society into a slight tremolo of confusion
and fright at least.

Individuals may order Green Integer titles through PayPal
www.paypal.com
Please pay the price listed below plus $2.00 for postage to Green
Integer through the PayPal system. You can also visit our site at
www.greeninteger.com
If you have questions please feel free to e-mail the publisher at
douglasmesserli@gmail.com
Bookstores and libraries should order through our distributors
USA and Canada: Consortium Book Sales
and Distribution/Perseus Books
United Kingdom and Europe: Turnaround Publisher Services
Unit 3, Olympia Trading Estate, Coburg Road, Wood Green,
London N22 6TZ UK

*

SELECTED POETRY TITLES

Press: 1-55713-304-2] $14.95

   *Shadowtime* [978-1-933382-00-5] $11.95

**Oswald Egger** *Room of Rumor: Tunings* [978-1-931243-66-7] $9.95

**Paul Éluard** *A Moral Lesson* [978-1-931243-95-7] $10.95

**Nikos Engonopoulos** *Acropolis and Tram: Poems 1938-1978* [978-1-933382-37-1] $13.95

**Federico García Lorca** *Suites* [1-892295-61-X] $12.95

**Peter Glassgold** *Hwæt!* [978-1-933382-41-8] $12.95

**Dieter M. Gräf** *Tousled Beauty* [978-1-933382-01-2] $11.95

   *Tussi Research* [978-1-933382-86-9] $13.96

**Hagiwara Sakutarō** *Howling at the Moon: Poems and Prose* [1-931243-01-8] $11.95

**Hsi Muren** *Across the Darkness of the River* [1-931243-24-7] $9.95

**Hsu Hui-chih** *Book of Reincarnation* [1-931243-32-8] $9.95

**Kim Soo-Bok** *Beating on Iron* [978-1-55713-430-1] $12.95

**Ko Un** *Himalaya Poems* [978-1-55713-412-7] $13.95

   *Songs for Tomorrow: Poems 1961-2001* [978-1-933382-70-8] $15.95

   *Ten Thousand Lives* [978-1-933382-06-7] $14.95

**Reiner Kunze** *Rich Catch in the Empty Creel* [978-1-933382-24-1] $15.95

**Lee Si-young** *Patterns* [978-1-55713-422-6] $11.95

**Lucebert** *The Collected Poems: Volume 1* [978-1-55713-407-3] $15.95

**Friederike Mayröcker** *with each clouded peak* [Sun & Moon Press: 1-55713-277-1] $11.95

**Deborah Meadows** *Representing Absence* [978-1-931243-77-3] $9.95

   *Thin Gloves* [978-1-933382-19-7] $12.95

**Douglas Messerli** *After* [Sun & Moon Press: 1-55713-353-0] $10.95

   *Bow Down* [ML&NLF: 1-928801-04-8] $12.95

   *First Words* [978-1-931243-41-4] $10.95

   *Dark* [978-1-933382-14-2] $12.95

   ed. *Listen to the Mockingbird: American Folksongs and Popular Music Lyrics of the 19th Century* [978-1-892295-20-0] $13.95

   *Maxims from My Mother's Milk/Hymns to Him: A Dialogue*

[Sun & Moon Press: 1-55713-047-7] $8.95

**Vítězslav Nezval** •*Antilyrik & Other Poems* [1-892295-75-X] $10.95

**Henrik Nordbrandt** *The Hangman's Lament: Poems* [978-1-931243-56-8] $10.95

**Antonio Porta** *Metropolis* [1-892295-12-1] $10.95

**Stephen Ratcliffe** *Sound / (system)* [1-931243-35-2] $12.95

**Elizabeth Robinson** *Pure Descent* [Sun & Moon Press: 1-55713-410-3] $10.95

**Reina María Rodríguez** *Violet Island and Other Poems* [978-1-892295-65-1] $12.95

**Gonzalo Rojas** *From the Lightning: Selected Poems* [978-1-933382-64-7] $14.95

**Jean-Pierre Rosnay** *When a Poet Sees a Chestnut Tree* [978-1-933382-20-3] $12.95

**Joe Ross** *EQUATIONS=equals* [978-1-931243-61-2] $10.95
  *Wordlick* [978-1-55713-415-8] $11.95

**Nelly Sachs** *Collected Poems 1944-1949* [978-1-933382-57-9] $13.95

**Paul Snoek** *Hercules Richelieu* and *Nostradamus* [1-892295-42-3] $10.95

  *The Song of Songs: Shir Hashirim* [1-931243-05-0] $9.95

**Adriano Spatola** *The Position of Things: Collected Poems 1961-1992* [978-1-933382-45-6] $15.95

**Takamura Kōtarō** *The Chieko Poems* [978-1-933382-75-3] $12.95

**Tomas Tranströmer** *The Sorrow Gondola* [978-1-933382-44-9] $11.95

**Paul van Ostaijen** *The First Book of Schmoll* [978-1933382-21-0] $12.95

**Xue Di** *Across Borders* [978-1-55713-423-3] $12.95

**Yang Lian** *Yi* [1-892295-68-7] $14.95

**Visar Zhiti** *The Condemned Apple: Selected Poetry* [978-1-931243-72-8] $10.95

# THE AMERICA AWARDS
*for a lifetime contribution to international writing*
Awarded by the Contemporary Arts Educational Project, Inc.
in loving memory of Anna Fahrni

The 2015 Award winner is:

EDWARD ALBEE [USA] 1928

*Previous winners:*

1994 Aimé Cesaire
[Martinique] 1913–2008

1995 Harold Pinter
[England] 1930–2008

1996 José Donoso [Chile] 1924-
1996 (*awarded prior to his death*)

1997 Friederike Mayröcker
[Austria] 1924

1998 Rafael Alberti
[Spain] 1902-1999

1999 Jacques Roubaud
[France] 1932

2000 Eudora Welty
[USA] 1909-2001

2001 Inger Christensen
[Denmark] 1935-2009

2002 Peter Handke [Austria] 1942

2003 Adonis (Ali Ahmad Said)
[Syria/Lebanon] 1930

2004 José Saramago
[Portugal] 1922-2010

2005 Andrea Zanzotto [Italy]
1921-2011

2006 Julien Gracq (Louis
Poirier) [France] 1910-2007

2007 Paavo Haavikko
[Finland] 1931

2008 John Ashbery [USA] 1927

2009 Günter Kunert
[GDR/Germany] 1929

2010 Javier Marías [Spain] 1951

2011 Ko Un [South Korea] 1933

2012 Ivo Michiels [Belgium] 1923

2013 Reiner Kunze
[GDR/Germany] 1933

2014 László Krasznahorkai
[Hungary] 1954